GET INTO
LAW

GET INTO LAW

Make your leap from student to solicitor

MEERA PATEL

Table of Contents

Introduction

Do you want to work as a lawyer? Are you applying for a legal internship? Have you already applied and want to know the secrets to success? I believe every aspiring student can make their journey from student to solicitor, you just need the map.

In the last few years many students have asked for my advice and mentoring on how to obtain a job in law and qualify as a UK solicitor. So, I have written this book to share with you my own personal blueprint and experience.

My learnings are through the lens of both a female and an ethnic minority, two groups, who in my view, should participate, represent and lead in the world of law more than ever. Why? Because through the act of claiming your place, you can empower yourself, and furthermore create positive change in the world we are living in today.

During this book you too will realise what led me to my "why" and how I made my leap, from studying law to qualified lawyer, working in London with a network of legal friends and global contacts.

As I look back, my younger self wished I could have picked up a book that gave me some inside tips. I will share these tips with you and candidly provide you with the exact steps to take for your success. Now you're ready to make your leap, this book is for you.

Let's navigate the path together through the next ten chapters. This journey is uniquely yours.

Companion Workbook

To guide you on your journey in making the leap from student to solicitor, this book will share with you effective practical actions.

Each chapter ends in key take-aways and in addition to this, a companion workbook can be found at the end. The workbook can be read alongside the book and kept for notetaking as you progress.

Chapter 1

Mindset is Everything

Whether you believe you can get a job in law or whether you believe you cannot - you are right. Developing a strong, focussed mindset is important as you start your journey. This is even more important if you are a woman, and furthermore, if you are an ethnic minority.

There can be narratives, statistics and people who will tell you that you may not make it, and if you do, you may not make it very far. Example narratives might include passing conversation that global law firm partners are predominantly privileged men, or learning that a friend (whom you believe is smarter than you) tried to get a job in law and now she does something else because the application process ended up being far too difficult.

Remember that the most important coach on your journey to get into law is YOU. Choose to engage in narratives that seek to propel you forward and use these as your own personal fuel.

During the time I applied for legal training contracts, whilst working towards my university law degree, I felt like I had two jobs. Quite possibly even three, as I had a part-time job in a clothing store. I would spend hours poring over law firm websites, trying to read (and vaguely comprehend) articles in the Financial Times and figure out the online legal job application processes. I would sit and wish that there was an easier way, or that once those first few job applications were completed all would be done. In the end, I realised that there are no shortcuts, and later learned that those first few job applications got rejected.

However, in that moment of receiving those three-line rejection emails instead of a law-firm welcome brochure, three key points became clear to me:

1. It is very rare for someone to get their first job in law from the first application they submit. At least one or two rejections are inevitable.

2. Do not waste the opportunity a rejection creates when it comes. Find out why you were rejected, and the specific actions you can take to improve.

3. Put in the work to improve.

The third point is perhaps the most important of the above. To help you improve you can often start with eliminating things that do not allow you to move forward. This includes mindless distractions, music that causes you to stop focusing and negativity from anyone around you.

Be mindful of what you are listening to and who you are listening to as you proceed on your journey.

It is helpful also to place yourself amongst conversations that enrich your path into law if these are not presented to you naturally. For example, if your friends or family do not talk about the latest articles in the Economist or the Lawyer, sign up for an online conference or listen to a podcast where useful topics in business and law are being discussed.

Your mindset and ability to remain resilient and confident will be essential every time you face a rejection, or if you feel like things are getting a little too tough. If your mindset is strong and focussed, you will have the best foundation to land your first job in law.

KEY TAKE-AWAYS

- Remove any narratives that are holding you back.
- Capitalise on rejections and see them as opportunities to grow yourself.
- Create an environment for mindset improvement.

Chapter 2

Knowing Yourself

Getting into the right mindset should come in tandem with knowing yourself. Knowing yourself is important because it will ensure that the direction you take is authentic to you as a person. Start by asking yourself: Why do I want to become a lawyer? This is a crucial question and if your "why" is not strong enough, you may find yourself struggling at the first hurdle.

During university I witnessed some of my peers opt to study Law at university because of status or because it was what their parents thought would be best for them. This type of reasoning is a dangerous "why" because it may not be strong enough for your ambitions to fully come to fruition. Part of my own "why" when I applied to study Law was because I wanted to understand the principles that underpinned society, and by having this, I could better effect positive change in the world.

Your "why" may be completely different from mine,

but is just as powerful to you. Take the time to clearly articulate this for yourself – it just needs to be a short and sweet statement and not an essay! Following this, try to understand what you think will be required of you to reach your "why".

Following the articulation of my "why," I swiftly realised that to graduate with a law degree I would perhaps have to work harder at university than many of my peers. This realisation was based on the significant amount of reading required, the need to memorise numerous cases and a real need for me to discipline myself to get the results I wanted. If my "why" and my understanding of what was required had not been strong or clear enough, I may have lost focus and desire.

As university progressed, I found myself coming back to my "why" again, and whilst I had studied Law at university, I asked myself this time why I wanted to qualify as a lawyer, and if I did want to qualify, where would I begin training? The requirements to qualify are that you will need a myriad of qualities. One quality is having excellent attention to detail – meticulous attention that you will not even believe existed within you. As a trainee solicitor, my supervisor told me the story of his own supervisor who told him to *"proofread a client document until his eyes bled."* This story is slightly extreme, and highlights the level of attention to detail that he felt was required. Another quality is the ability to read copious amounts of information and distil this all down to the key points with enough evidence to back up every point you make.

As you proceed on your journey, you may trip up if you begin to make points that you cannot back up – this really applies from the interview all the way to drafting up pieces of research and important client emails. By putting on a veneer or making a superfluous point, you can do yourself a disservice and instead can be better positioned by putting in the work and research time to substantiate what you want to say. This can be hard, but refer back to Chapter 1, Mindset is Everything.

I realised that I wanted to develop these qualities and I knew that if anything, by qualifying as a lawyer, I would possess some valuable skills for life. For example, you will become a pro at writing complaint letters, you will find yourself identifying flaws in arguments incredibly quickly and you will relish trawling through reams of documentation to establish facts that others may not even attempt to touch because they may feel overwhelmed.

As my "why" and understanding of the related requirements started to develop, I looked at the type of law firm I would want to work at. For this part, it is as simple as asking yourself key questions such as, *do I like large, corporate environments or smaller, family-like environments? What types of clients do I want to work with – individuals, small companies, or large listed companies? What type of people do I get along with? What interests me and does that law firm have a record of nurturing people in that area,* (for example your specific niche could be intellectual property, data privacy or technology)? It is important to be honest with yourself. It is incredibly common for students to not ask these questions first and send out a scattergun of applications to many law firms. Do not get drawn to the big firms just because of a brand name if it is not what you truly want.

KEY TAKE-AWAYS

- Clearly articulate for yourself why you want to study law and why you want to qualify as a lawyer.
- Define specific factors for the type of firm you want to work at and qualify with.
- Be honest as you ask these questions of yourself.

Chapter 3

Market Research

I n my first year of studying Law at university, a friend suggested I attend our university's law fair as he had heard that the big law firms were showcasing themselves and then handing out some great freebies. Apparently even the first-year Geography students were feigning interest in a legal career for a free pen, umbrella or USB stick. I was intrigued, so I attended, and I came back to my student residence that day with a bag of goodies. Did I make the most of this law fair? No. Had I asked myself at this point what kind of job in law I truly wanted and why? No. However, I did get a flavour for the types of law firms and associated branding that existed.

In my second year, I went back to my university's annual law fair. However, this time round I was intentional about my approach. What was valuable to me in my second year was speaking to the people that stood behind each stall – I had also developed my confidence to have these conversations. The knowledge and experience I gained from attending was valuable, and unsurprisingly, the previous enticement of a free pen was of little interest. In my second year, I looked deeply at the type of culture, the people-exposure, and opportunities the law firms would offer me. I had also started to know myself better and thought about which firm would match my values and where I thought I would best fit. I asked questions of trainee solicitors and partners who stood behind the stalls, such as, *"Why did you join this particular law firm?"*, *"What is the best and worst thing you have experienced at your law firm?"* and *"Does your law firm offer international secondments?"*

Knowing the market involves researching different types of law firms, understanding various cultures attached to those law firms, and finding out what each firm can specifically offer you. Your ability to know yourself will also start to increase as you research the market more – you will notice this as certain firms will instinctively put you off (and you know **exactly** why). Another key indicator of a good fit is when two similar law firms may be equally interesting to you, but one draws you in more based on something specific to you or a few facts you have learned about the firm that resonate with you.

It is vital to spend time knowing yourself in order to correlate, connect with and draw appropriate conclusions from your market research. For example, if you know you like small teams, international opportunity, and a fast pace, then specific law firms will appeal to you. Those law firms may not appeal or be suited to someone else who likes medium sized teams, regional work, and perhaps a better work-life balance. By connecting knowing yourself with your law firm, business and/or company market research, you are at a distinct advantage because you are entering the legal recruitment market with clear direction that will enable you to find a role in law best-suited to you.

KEY TAKE-AWAYS

- Be intentional in your approach when attending law firm events and university law fairs.
- Prepare valuable questions that can help you better understand the legal recruitment market.
- Know yourself and connect this to your market research, to draw conclusions.

Chapter 4

Connections, Connections, Connections

I was the first person in my family to go to university, and unsurprisingly the first to think about applying to a top-rated university to study Law with the aspiration of becoming a lawyer. When I was applying to university, I did not know anyone who was a "big-city lawyer", nor did I get introduced to anyone in these circles during the initial stages of my journey by chance.

Law is still a profession where who you know can count for a lot. This became apparent to me as I observed individuals securing informal work experience to having a personal connection mentor them through the career application process. If you do not have any legal professional connections and you are starting from scratch, you are going to need to utilise all the tools in your existing armoury - and to do this gracefully, in a way that leaves you looking professional.

I was recently approached by a university student, let's refer to her as Jane, who was looking for legal work experience or a role as a paralegal. She had sent out numerous job applications online, secured a few interviews but had ultimately faced rejection. Alongside this, Jane really did not know anyone in the world of law to ask for guidance and was working hard during her final year at university.

We worked on developing her mindset to build resiliency (see Chapter 1, Mindset is Everything), took some time to ask questions to help her know herself (see Chapter 2, Knowing Yourself), and she diligently researched the legal market to see where she would fit best (see Chapter 3, Market Research). Following this process, Jane realised she had to be bold and professional in how she developed and built her legal network to locate job opportunities. Jane started to make use of professional LinkedIn networking, alongside attending law firm open days and events.

We live in an era of professional social media networking, and anyone is one message away from a response that could lead to your first foot in the door. Jane searched for professionals on LinkedIn that inspired her, or that she could see herself work shadowing or assisting. I asked her to craft a short note to each person introducing herself and expressing her interest in what they did and asking if they had time for a short conversation regarding career advice. Her note was professional, polite and concise. I reminded her to check her spelling and grammar – REMEMBER, lawyers do not look favourably upon spelling errors! Jane then checked that her introduction notes came across as professional and keen, instead of weird and stalker-like.

I reminded her that the reality is that if she sent ten notes out, one or maybe no-one may reply to her, but she should not allow the lack of responses to deter her. She received no replies to her first eight messages that she sent out. However, a few weeks later, she received a reply from a prominent intellectual property lawyer who offered her time to talk about the company she worked at, provided her with useful information, and described the potential work experience and paralegal opportunities Jane could apply for at the company. She could not believe this person ACTUALLY replied to her message and gave her a route to a job opportunity. She diligently followed up with this contact and her associated HR team for a further conversation and received advice on how to apply for potential roles at the company.

Another avenue you may want to explore are law firm open days and legal events. You could aim to follow up with the organiser who might be able to introduce you to a suitable mentor within their network, a speaker from the event, or a trainee solicitor to find out more about a particular law firm. Every time you build a professional connection with someone new in the world of law, ask them to introduce you to someone else who you would also find it interesting to connect with and repeat this ask with the next person. By the time you have done this a few times over, you will have a handful of people whom you can call or email if you need informal advice on your journey. You will find that there are lots of people who will want to help you if you are polite and have a positive attitude.

Legal recruiters can be an excellent group of people to speak with. They will not only know the job market but can also advise you on the latest paralegal roles. Further, they can keep you updated and let you know of the law firms that are actively looking to hire a candidate just like you.

One area I have witnessed students struggle with is that of making and developing a new connection. It can often feel awkward or perhaps intimidating to connect on areas of mutual interest outside of the law. For example, conversational topics such as wine tasting, rugby or weekends in the Alps may be topics you are not particularly well-versed in. Do not allow this to deter you, and although your initial conversation may not be as fluid as you'd hoped because you have no idea where the ski-resort your new connection just mentioned is, remember that ultimately people always find something to connect on. You should not shy away or pretend to be something that you are not just to "fit in". Simply acknowledge and show interest in their interests and in due time, a topic of mutual interest will arise.

KEY TAKE-AWAYS

- Build your legal network early.
- Ask one connection to introduce you to one or two others and build from there.
- Utilise LinkedIn, open days and legal events to increase your network and opportunities.

Chapter 5

The Devil is in the Detail

During the application process, I observed two girls whom I knew – let's refer to them as Sienna and Yan. Sienna put together and sent out over fifty online applications for training contracts and legal roles and received zero offers. Yan sent out only ten online applications for training contracts and legal roles and received three training contract offers.

Sienna and Yan spent similar amounts of time putting together their job applications. I remember thinking that Sienna obviously had a better chance of getting a job offer, and that she must have spent more time on her job applications than Yan. In time, however, I realised the difference between Sienna and Yan's chances of success depended on how closely they paid attention to the details of their targeted law firms when putting together their applications. Sienna did not spend time on this or realise its importance, but Yan did.

Hiring managers and those involved in the recruitment process at law firms want to know that you think they and their firm are special.

They look to see that specific, tailored effort has been made by you in your application. The moment I realised this, everything changed from the way I crafted a job application to how I approached an interview. Law firms want to know that you have taken the time to research what they are good at and why. Did they win an award for a particular piece of work they carried out for a well-known client? Do they have an excellent track record for pro-bono work? Be sure to mention these types of specifics in your application, because not only will this give you a talking point at a first interview, but it will show that you made the requisite effort to tailor your application to a particular firm. As a result, that firm will think that you in turn might also be right for them.

To bring this all together, and bringing in Chapter 2, you also need to circle back to the "Know Yourself" part and why you as an individual connect with these specifics about the firm. For example, I applied to a law firm that was well known for hiring diverse candidates and candidates who had an entrepreneurial nature. In my application I called out why those two specific points connected with me personally, and why I admired this attribute of the firm.

This careful detailing is the difference between an *average* application and a **good** one – and trust me hiring managers can tell who has put in the effort and who has not! A hiring manager may be thinking that if you cannot demonstrate putting in the effort to find out the specifics of a firm on your job application, how much effort are you going to put in when they hire you to work at the firm? Remember, competition for training contracts and legal roles can be fierce. If you do not put in the effort to research the details from the law firm or company website, there will be someone else who will illustrate this neatly in their application. You want to ensure you are being looked at favourably alongside those who take the extra step. Do not place yourself at an early disadvantage when bringing out the details on your application is completely within your control.

KEY TAKE-AWAYS

- Research specific facts that draw you to your target law firms or company.

- Illustrate how those specific facts resonate with you and why you are applying in your applications.

- Consider the number of applications you make because quality counts over quantity.

Chapter 6

The Makings of a Good CV

Your CV, or curriculum vitae, is your "hello" to a recruiter, hiring manager or interviewer. You should want that "hello" to be impressive, tailored to the person reading it, and make them want to have a conversation (i.e. arrange an interview).

Whilst many students are comfortable putting together a basic CV, for example including key headings such as Profile, Academic Record, Work Experience, Employment, Languages, Achievements and Interests, and compiling all the information necessary under those headings, it truly does take a bit more work to upgrade it to a great, interview-ready CV.

If you are not quite there yet and are starting from a blank Word document, do some online research and find yourself a CV template to download. There are hundreds available, so find one that looks clean, professional and contains similar headings to the above.

Over the last few years, I have supported students in reviewing their CVs and often whilst their initial draft is fine, it can usually be improved. I realised that many students find it helpful to understand how their CV can be improved. Below are my top ten points to consider when upgrading your CV.

1. Keep your CV to two pages on a Word document – anything longer risks not being concise, and the reader will lose interest.

2. Check your spelling and grammar three times – use online tools or automatic spell-checkers as many times as required.

3. Keep your language and tone professional. Avoid using humour or colloquial phrases.

4. Make sure your formatting is consistent. This includes ensuring you are using either right-align or centre-align consistently and making sure you are using exactly the same type of bullet point and indentation consistently throughout your document.

5. Upgrade vague skill phrases to be more precise. For example, "Can work as part of a team" could be improved to "Worked as part of a 4-person team to organise a charity event that raised £1,000."

6. Use key phrases that show why you would be right for that specific law-firm or company. For example, you could include, "Researched and drafted a paper on the impact of GDPR" if you are applying to a

company that has a data-privacy legal department.

7. Include evidence of where you have undertaken activities to develop yourself in the world of law. For example, "Attended and networked at a legal technology event. Followed up and further discussed artificial intelligence and law with the event's key speakers."

8. Insert figures or values if you can. For example, "Built a spreadsheet to determine the cost of a summer event" could be upgraded to "Led financial calculations and built a spreadsheet for a budgeted £5,000 university event in June."

9. Include legal job competency words within your relevant examples. Examples of legal competency words include analytical skills, logic and reasoning, writing ability, business acumen, clear communication, and professional networking.

10. Find your personal way to stand out from the crowd. Have you led your university dance society? Are you volunteering for a mental health charity? Did you train consistently for a marathon or a triathlon? All of these examples will display a certain quality that is unique to you and demonstrates a transferrable skillset to a legal environment.

In addition to the information described above, legal recruiters and recruitment websites typically have good articles and tips on how to improve your CV for the legal recruitment market. You should not be afraid to ask a legal recruiter how you could improve your CV to ensure you have a better chance of obtaining a certain role. A good recruiter will provide some helpful pointers and suggestions, as they will have seen thousands of CVs over the course of their day-to-day.

KEY TAKE-AWAYS

- Utilise the top ten points above to upgrade your CV.

- Ask legal recruiters for pointers and tips to ensure your CV fits the grade for the role you are applying for.

- Always tailor your CV to every individual job.

Chapter 7

What is "Commercial Awareness"?

In Chapter 1, Mindset is Everything, I shared with you the importance of asking for feedback when you are rejected by a law firm or company. During my application process I asked for feedback from a kind lady in HR who told me that I needed to improve my "commercial awareness". At this point in time, following my first interview, I had no idea what was meant by "commercial awareness".

I was incredibly glad I asked and pushed for that feedback because it really changed the game for me. Commercial awareness does not happen overnight, and by consistently working on my commercial awareness skills, I was able to really excel in the interviews I attended going forward. I truly believe anyone can build commercial awareness, and I will describe my exact methodology on how I did this in this chapter.

To begin with, and to clarify what commercial is - it is the ability to be up-to-speed on business and world news and apply this to how a law firm operates and serves its clients. It is important because solicitors will typically advise their clients on issues related to business, economic or political events. Having the attribute of commercial awareness can be the difference between succeeding at an interview or not.

To develop your commercial awareness, ask yourself what articles, journals, or other materials you should be making an extra effort to read that you have not already read. I decided to start reading the Economist, Time magazine, and the Financial Times. These publications, especially the Economist and the Financial Times are lengthy, and you would not be best served trying to read every single page like you would read a book. Start by scanning the headings and find the articles that are at the top of the global and UK business agenda, and secondly find articles relevant to your area of legal interest.

For example, areas of daily business news that have significant impact on business at the time of writing this book include Brexit, and when I graduated from university in 2009, it was the Financial Crisis. Areas that could be significant to you if you are applying to a firm that specialises in corporate mergers and acquisitions may include a recent M&A deal in a specific industry sector. Over time, these articles will become easier to read, and you will be able to track and follow certain stories with interest.

When I first started reading the Financial Times at university I found the language and content fairly difficult to digest. I grew up in a family that did not read the Financial Times daily and I remember feeling at the time that only "posh" or "wealthy" people read the FT – anyone who grew up in a similar way may relate to this. At the time, I had concocted this clear image of men wearing pinstripe suits sitting on the train reading this sprawling pink paper – an image I could not personally relate to. This resulted in me shying away from and almost feeling embarrassed to read this business paper. I shared my struggles with a university professor who suggested that sometimes you can find the same business news stories more succinctly and plainly written in another newspaper. He suggested I start by reading the business section of the Evening Standard. I did, and at last, business news stories I could understand.

After a few months of reading the business section of the Evening Standard, I went back to the Financial Times, and things started to feel somewhat easier and I strangely started to enjoy reading a paper I once thought only "posh and wealthy pin-stripe suit wearing types" liked to read. For those of you who are struggling to read dense business news stories straightaway, take bite size steps. Ultimately it is much better to understand the article you are reading than to read an article in its entirety and not comprehend it. In addition to reading specific publications geared towards building my commercial awareness, I also started to watch business television channels such as Bloomberg. To keep up to date with daily business news, you should find the most helpful mediums that work for you. For example, you may prefer to regularly listen to a podcast.

And just when all that extra reading you may have thought, on top of your university reading, is all that it takes - this is only the first step in building your commercial awareness. It is the next step which gets you to the heart of showcasing your ability to work as a solicitor. This step is to apply the business news stories to the operations of the law firm or company you are applying to.

I will illustrate how this is done by providing an indicative example: You read a business story on how the UK is exiting the European Union and the fact that certain EU laws may no longer apply in the UK. This is going to impact and be relevant across various departments of a law firm. For example, in relation to competition, merger and antitrust cases handled by the European Commission could instead be subject to parallel reviews by the European Commission and the UK competition authority. In relation to corporate, the impact of the UK's exit could lead global businesses to review how they operate and trade cross-border. In relation to employment, this could impact HR processes and business travel at clients and at the law firm itself. Here is a clear three-step methodology you can apply:

1. Read, watch or listen and truly comprehend the business news story at hand.

2. Write down a list of key departments at the law-firm or company you are applying to – for example Tax, Corporate, Litigation, Employment.

3. Assess the news story against each department and ask pertinent questions including:

- How will this story impact each department's clients?

- How will this story impact each department itself?

- Is the impact good or bad?

- Could the news story lead to a profit or loss for the company or law firm?

Every time you read a business article, listen to a podcast, or watch a piece of business news, go through and apply this methodology either in your mind, or write down notes – this is how you develop your commercial awareness.

KEY TAKE-AWAYS

- Make a list of legal or business publications to subscribe to and regularly access the content.
- With dense and lengthy publications it is often easier to comprehend them by taking bite size steps.
- The three-step methodology in this chapter can be applied to develop your commercial awareness.

Chapter 8

The Interview is Just the Start

An interview is the place where you can bring together all your preparation to sell yourself to a law firm or company.

I can vividly remember my first interview for a law-firm summer vacation scheme. Prior to the interview I was stressing with my flatmate specifically in relation to what to wear to the interview. I learned that finding the right balance of professional and being yourself is key. Women are fortunate in many ways because we do not have to wear a suit to get this right – a smart, conservative dress, or a smart skirt and top can work just fine. For men, suits are usually the go-to, and I observed a male friend receive advice to not wear a colourful tie. He was told that, *"Until the rules of the game change, keep the colourful ties at home!"* You also do not have to spend a fortune on what you wear, and high street brands will suffice. Ensure your clothes are clean, ironed, fit well and you feel comfortable in them. It is a good idea to show your interview outfit to a person you can trust, to make sure you are striking the right professional tone. Interviews are the place where judgement can take place well before you even open your mouth! First impressions are everything.

In addition to the classic wardrobe dilemma, some students impress when interviewing for a part-time job outside of law however can switch in persona when applying for a legal job. The underlying cause for this switch is that they often take the legal job interview much more seriously and occasionally think they need to be a completely different person for the interview – a more intelligent, serious and "*lawyer-like*" person.

The truth is that you should be just as confident when interviewing for a part-time job as you are when interviewing for a legal job. It is often the character-development activities and traits developed within the context of a part-time job that are transferable to a legal job and make you an even stronger candidate. If you resonate with this and have a part-time job, practice providing evidence of your transferable skills from your part-time job to a legal role, and use these examples to give yourself even more confidence.

One way to help overcome any fears and increase your preparation is to attend mock-interviews. Ask your university or college if they provide mock law firm interviews or search online for reputable places that can provide this. In addition, try listing out sample interview questions on flashcards and ask a friend to run through them with you.

In my view, a good answer to an interview question has two core components – it is well-structured and provides the right amount of detail. Well-structured answers are logical – so, make a point, provide supporting evidence, and draw a conclusion. Always be prepared to back up any points you make! The right amount of detail component allows you to show your depth of thinking as you do this. You can aim to include specificity in your answers with examples, supporting data sources or figures. As a guide, you may be providing too much detail if you find yourself rambling and/or using vague language – you could try to record yourself to see if you sit on the wrong or right side of detail! Keep practicing until you get the balance right.

Another must-do prior to an interview is to think of questions you can ask your interviewers. This can be a quick win because you can prepare a list of ten potential questions you could ask, and select two or three on the day, depending on how the conversation flows. Good questions to ask can vary from a question specifically for the interviewer, such as, *"Why did you join the firm?"* or *"You are listed as working on this M&A deal, what did you learn from this and why was it an interesting transaction?"* to general questions about what your experience at the firm or company may look like, such as *"Does the company provide international opportunities at a junior level?"* or *"How diverse is the leadership within the company?"*

When the day of your interview finally draws near, it is useful to re-read your application, figure out your travel routes (if the interview is not online!), and leave enough time to arrive early. Get a good night's sleep and allow your confidence and preparation to carry you towards making an excellent impression. After the interview, always thank the interviewers for their time. A bonus tip - if you can send the interviewers a short, polite email within 24 hours of your interview to thank them, you should!

KEY TAKE-AWAYS

- First impressions count. Your outfit should reflect who you are and at the same time be appropriate for a professional workplace.
- Use mock interviews to practice and prepare structured, "right amount of detail" answers.
- Prepare questions in advance to ask your interviewers.

Chapter 9

Careers Do Not Run in Straight Lines

Life up until you enter the world of work can often seem like you're taking a path that's already been prepared for you – by this I mean, you go to school, you take your exams, then you go to university. If you've followed this path until now, your next steps may be that you apply for internships, or you apply for a job. Even if you are fortunate enough to get the first job you apply for, careers following this often do not run in straight lines.

My personal experience was that whilst school and university had prepared me academically, I received little preparational support in relation to the working world, and even less guidance on how to build a career once I got my first job.

I was fortunate to land a legal training contract following university. However, following my first full-time job in the city, I really had to teach myself how to build a career that was unique to my strengths and one that was authentic and rewarding to me.

As I started my training contract, I met students who struggled to make the leap from student to the world of work. I noticed that this was sometimes tied to linear thinking about how to get a job in law (and this is not surprising given the pre-planned path most students walk, as described earlier).

It was those who thought outside of the box who often landed excellent roles or made great career moves. For example, if you are struggling to obtain a legal role in the UK, why not look to British Overseas Territories such as Gibraltar, the Cayman Islands, Bermuda, or the British Virgin Islands. During my days as a student, a friend, who we can refer to as Dia, was struggling to obtain a legal training contract. We had graduated during the financial crisis in 2009 and training contracts were increasingly difficult to secure. Instead of wallowing, Dia applied for and secured a paralegal role in Turks and Caicos. As I sat at my desk in rainy London, I scrolled through her photos on social media after she had left the UK, and there she was with her fellow paralegals on the beach after work - I could not help but think she'd made a great move personally and professionally! On returning to the UK, Dia found that she had built up enough paralegal experience and legal knowledge in Turks and Caicos to secure a London-based training contract quickly and easily.

As I write this book, we are finding the world of work moving towards video-conferencing and full-time remote work. Even if a company is based in another UK or overseas location that you cannot reasonably commute to, it is always a good idea to ask if the role can be worked remotely. If the role can be worked remotely, this will provide you with yet another route or option.

If moving abroad to a beach town or a remote working role does not appeal to you, then think even further outside of the box. For example, if you have an interest in data privacy law, why not apply for an internship or junior role within the data-privacy team of a technology company or start-up? This experience and knowledge can serve you well if you then decide to apply for a training contract at a firm that specialises in data-privacy and technology.

There is a proverb that goes something like, "If at first you don't succeed, try, try again." Whilst this phrase is useful, I think in the world of law, you need to be strategic if after several tries things are not working for you. It is perhaps best to try again, but also to think outside of the box and to not limit yourself to a linear path.

I can assure you that life will test you if you remain on a linear path that is not authentic to you. Build your career in a way that is truly unique and powerful for you.

KEY TAKE-AWAYS

- Think outside of the box.
- Consider all your options – work abroad, work remotely, work in a different UK location or work in an area aligned to law.
- Build a career that is authentic to you.

Chapter 10

The Future is Yours

The world of law is ever-evolving and over the last ten years I have seen traditional legal-service models be redefined. Whilst thinking outside of the box can be one avenue to increase your career options, having an eye on the future is another.

Being able to grasp and understand legal concepts that will have increasing importance in five years' time is strategically useful for you. This is because you will be able to ascertain and can then decide to develop an area of expertise that will be new to the legal market, and therefore position yourself quickly as an authority once working. I have observed this in relation to lawyers who chose to focus on areas such as technology, intellectual property and data privacy ten years ago. Today, they are in high demand due to their niche-specific skills and in-demand expertise.

Key market trends for you to be aware of include the intersection of technology and law. For example, take a look into bespoke technology training contracts, legal innovation roles, and job opportunities with machine learning contract analysis companies.

Another trend is sustainability, which includes the legal aspects of environmental policy and global sustainability strategy. Both technology and sustainability in my view are areas that will be vital to our global future and it is only logical to think that these areas will need bright legal minds to navigate and shape evolving legislation.

We are also seeing true globalisation of the legal practice with UK law firms seeking to be more involved in locations such as Africa, India and Latin America. For students with ethnic minority backgrounds and students having a connection to these countries, the opportunity to get involved may appeal as you will have the unique ability to understand cultural sensitivities and nuances, and you may also have the right language skills to navigate this market.

True gender representation and diversity has now become a mandate for many law firms and businesses. For women and ethnic minorities, many businesses are subscribing to the fact that diversity can equal profitability. If you do not see anyone in a leadership position at the place you are applying to that looks like you – remember that you are the future. And YOU can create the blueprint for those who come after you.

KEY-TAKEAWAYS

- Be aware of market trends (i.e. technology and sustainability) and how these link to law.

- Research UK law firms who are growing their global practice areas.

- Diversity and inclusion are increasingly a mandate for businesses – YOU are the future.

Epilogue

I hope this book has spoken to you and supports your journey, and that the personal stories I have shared help you to navigate your path from student to solicitor.

Your path is unique to you. Create the future you desire. As you make your leap and achieve your goals, aim to help those who follow in your footsteps.

GET INTO LAW

Make your leap from student to solicitor

Companion Workbook

MEERA PATEL

CHAPTER 1
Mindset is Everything

Action Items:

1. What are the top three things you can do today to create an improved mindset environment for yourself?

1	
2	
3	

2. Write down a job application that resulted in rejection, the feedback you received and the actions you have taken or will take to improve.

Application Made	
Feedback Received	
Improvement Actions	

CHAPTER 2
Knowing Yourself

Action Items:

1. Write down your answers to the following questions in bullets or short sentences, as applicable.

    a) Why do you want to study law?

    b) Why do you want to qualify as a lawyer

a)	
b)	

2. What type of work environment suits you best? Think about workplace culture, nature of the work, number of people in a team, working hours, etc. List out your top three desires from a working environment.

1	
2	
3	

CHAPTER 3
Market Research

Action Items:

1. Be honest and ask yourself how well you know the current legal job market. Write down a list of five pre-prepared questions to ask at law fairs, open days, and when in conversation with legal professionals.

1	
2	
3	
4	
5	

CHAPTER 4
Connections, Connections, Connections

Action Items:

1. Make a list of your current legal professional connections. Ask them to introduce you to three more people in their network. If you do not have any existing legal connections, schedule three law events you can attend with the sole purpose of building your legal network.

1	
2	
3	

2. Follow up and keep in touch with your new and existing legal connections and develop your network.

CHAPTER 5
The Devil is in the Detail

Action Items:

1. Read through your job applications and ask yourself if specific tailoring and detail has been applied to each application.

2. If required, tailor your applications further.

CHAPTER 6
The Makings of a Good CV

Action Items:

1. Cross-check and upgrade your CV against the top ten points listed in Chapter 6, The Makings of a Good CV.

2. Ask for feedback on your CV from a trusted professional and legal recruiter.

3. Aim to tailor your CV to specific roles and save different versions.

CHAPTER 7
What is "Commercial Awareness?"

Action Items:

1. Give yourself a rating from 1 – 10 on your level of "commercial awareness".

2. Take daily actions to improve your commercial awareness, including reading business news stories, listening to business podcasts and engaging in business/legal-focused conversations. Aim to apply the three-step methodology in Chapter 7, What is "Commercial Awareness", as you go.

3. Following three months of undertaking *these* daily actions, give yourself a rating from 1 – 10 again. Has your rating improved? Ask yourself why or why not?

CHAPTER 8
The Interview is Just the Start

Action Items:

1. Prepare your own answers to common law firm interview questions and arrange a mock-interview to test your interview skills.

2. Flag areas for your personal improvement and discuss these with your mock interviewer.

CHAPTER 9
Careers Do Not Run in Straight Lines

Action Items:

1. Brainstorm, research, and discuss job ideas beyond applying for a training contract.

2. Make a list below, and also on your phone, to remind yourself of the many options and routes to your desired goal of obtaining a legal role.

1	
2	
3	
4	
5	

CHAPTER 10
The Future is Yours

Action Items:

1. Identify 3-5 key business and legal market trends. Take time to research each trend and write down links between each trend and the role you are applying for.

Business Trend	Link to Role
Technology	
Sustainability	
Diversity and Inclusion	

Printed in Great Britain
by Amazon

84087606R00041